NINJA FOODi POSSIBLECOOKER PRO COOKBOOK FOR BEGINNERS

1100 days of step by step simple homemade recipes to slow cook, sear/saute, braise, sous vide, bake, steam and more

Nancy C. Bergstrom

DISCLAIMER

This book is an independent publication and is not endorsed, sponsored, or affiliated with the manufacturer of Ninja products. All recipes and instructions provided in this book are based on the author's own research, experiences, and opinions. The recipes and information contained in this book are for general guidance only and are not intended to be medical or nutritional advice. By using this book, you agree to hold harmless the author, publisher, and any other parties involved in the creation and distribution of this book from any damages or liabilities resulting from your use of the recipes and information contained herein."

NINJA Foodi

POSSIBLECOOKER PRO

COOKBOOK FOR BEGINNERS

1100 Days of step by step simple homemade recipes to slow cook, sear/saute, braise, sous vide, bake, steam and more.

NINJA MEAL PLANNER

Weekly. Guided. Planning

GET YOUR BONUS

Turn to the last page to claim your bonus

WHAT YOU'LL FIND IN THIS BOOK :

STEP 1:

Introduction

WHAT IS NINJA FOODI POSSIBLE COOKER
- Benefit
- Functions
- Getting Started
- **General Safety Instructions**
- **Cleaning and Maintenance**

WHAT IS NINJA FOODI POSSIBLE COOKER

The Ninja Foodi PossibleCooker PRO is an 8-in-1 multicooker that can replace 14 kitchen appliances. It is a versatile and powerful appliance that can help you save time and money in the kitchen.

BENEFIT

Saves Time and Money: The Ninja Foodi PossibleCooker PRO cooks food up to 30% faster than a conventional oven, and it can replace 14 kitchen appliances, so you can save money on counter space and storage.

Versatile: You can cook a wide variety of meals with the Ninja Foodi PossibleCooker PRO, from hearty stews and roasted vegetables to crispy air-fried snacks and decadent desserts.

Easy to Use: The controls are simple and intuitive, and the included recipe guide provides inspiration for delicious meals.

Healthy Cooking: The Ninja Foodi PossibleCooker PRO allows you to cook with less oil and butter, so you can enjoy healthier meals without sacrificing flavor.

Easy to Clean: The nonstick pot and dishwasher-safe parts make cleanup easy

FUNCTIONS

SLOW COOK: Slow cook after pushing the power button turn the control dial to select slow cook this is where the ninja will act like a slow cooker to cook your food at a lower temperature but for a longer period of time follow the recipe instructions, there are only two temperature settings for slow cook low or high so set low or high based on the recipe then select the cook time slow cook low time may be adjusted between 6 and 12 hours, slow cook High may be adjusted between 3 and 12 hours, after you place your ingredients in the pot and set the temperature and cook time press the start button to begin slow cooking the LCD will begin to count down the cook time when the cook time reaches zero the foodi will beep and will automatically switch to keep warm and the LCD will begin counting up so that you know how long the foodi has been keeping your food warm.

SEAR/SAUTE: With this setting you use the foodi as a stovetop for Browning meats sauteed veggies and simmering sauces there are only two temperature settings with sear/saute; low or high allow the foodi to heat up for five minutes prior to adding food to the pot when using the sear/saute setting you cannot set a countdown cooking time in the sear saute setting however after you press the start button the LCD will count up so that you know how long the sear/saute setting has been on do not use metal utensils with the foodi pot, metal utensils will scratch the non-stick coating on the pot, you can use the sear/saute taste setting with or without the glass lid placed on the pot.

STEAM: Use steam to cook delicate Foods at a high temperature when using steam you cannot set the temperature but you can set the cooking time you need to add one or more cups of water when using steam after you add the water and the food to steam press the start button the foodi will start a preheating and PrE will appear on the LCD after the water starts to boil the cooking time will start to count down when the cook time counts down to zero the foodi will beep and end will appear in the LCD then the foodi will automatically switch to keep warm and the LCD will begin to count up so that you know how long the foodi has been in the keep warm mode.

KEEP WARM: Keep warm to keep your food warm after it has been cooked you cannot set the temperature but you can set a keep warm time up to six hours.

SOUS VIDE: Sous vide the process of cooking food that has been vacuum sealed and you cook that food while it's in that vacuum sealed bag in a temperature controlled bath water this foodi provides that temperature controlled bath water.

BRAISE: Braise is used to transform tougher cuts of meat by first Browning it at high heat with oil and then simmering it in liquid at low heat this is a two-step process with this foodi first you will use the sear/saute setting to Brown the meat at a high temperature then you will use the braise setting to simmer the heat in a liquid at low heat.

BAKE: Is used to bake several different things, you can use bake as the primary setting or as a secondary setting in a two-step process with the bake setting you can set a temperature range between 250 and 425 degrees Fahrenheit you can set a bake time up to six hours press the start stop button to begin baking when the cook time reaches zero the foodi will beep and display end on the LCD for five minutes if the food requires more cook time use the time Arrow buttons to add more time.

PROOF: Is for proofing dough if you want to make your own bread proofing is a step in the preparation of yeast bread and other baked goods in which before baking, dough is allowed to rest and Rise.

GETTING STARTED

Unboxing and Setup: Carefully unpack your Ninja Foodi PossibleCooker PRO and remove all packaging materials. Wash the pot, lid, and any other removable parts with warm, soapy water and dry thoroughly before first use.

Choose the Right Function: Decide on the cooking method you want to use.
The PossibleCooker PRO offers eight functions: Slow Cook, Sear/Sauté, Sous side, Steam, Bake, Roast, Proof, and Keep Warm.

Add Ingredients: Place your ingredients in the pot, ensuring they don't exceed the maximum fill line

Set Cooking Time and Temperature: Select the desired cooking time and temperature using the control panel. Adjust the settings as needed for your chosen recipe.

Start Cooking: Press the Start/Stop button to begin the cooking process. The display will show the remaining cooking time.

Monitor Progress: Keep an eye on your food during cooking to ensure it's cooking evenly and to the desired doneness. if necessary, You may need to adjust the cooking time or temperature.

Flip or Stir (if required): For some cooking methods, such as Sear/Sauté you may need to flip or stir your food midway through cooking to ensure even cooking

End of Cooking Cycle: When the cooking cycle is complete, the PossibleCooker PRO will beep and switch to the Keep Warm function.

Transfer Food (if necessary): If you're transferring your food to a serving dish, use oven mitts to handle the hot pot and lid.

Enjoy Your Meal: Savor your delicious home-cooked meal.

GENERAL SAFETY INSTRUCTIONS

- Always unplug the PossibleCooker PRO from the power outlet when not in use.
- Never leave the PossibleCooker PRO unattended while it is in operation.
- Do not touch the hot surfaces of the PossibleCooker PRO, including the pot, lid, and handles. However, Use oven mitts when handling hot components
- Do not place the PossibleCooker PRO on or near a hot stovetop or open flame.
- Do not immerse the PossibleCooker PRO in water or any other liquid.
- Do not use metal utensils in the pot, as they may scratch the nonstick coating. Use wooden or silicone utensils instead.
- Do not fill the pot beyond the maximum fill line.
- Do not overfill the pot, as this could cause spills and splatters.
- Do not place any objects on top of the PossibleCooker PRO while it is in operation.
- Do not use the PossibleCooker PRO for any purpose other than cooking.

CLEANING AND MAINTENANCE

- Always allow the PossibleCooker PRO to cool completely before cleaning.
- However, Wash the pot, lid, and other removable parts with warm, soapy water.
- The nonstick pot is dishwasher-safe. However, hand washing is recommended for optimal results and to extend the life of the nonstick coating.
- Do not use abrasive cleaners, scouring pads, or harsh chemicals to clean the PossibleCooker PRO.
- Wipe the exterior of the PossibleCooker PRO with a damp cloth.
- Dry all parts thoroughly before storing the PossibleCooker PRO.

BREAKFAST

BREAKFAST BISCUITS & GRAVY

Prep: 5mins. Cook Time: 30mins. SERVINGS: 5

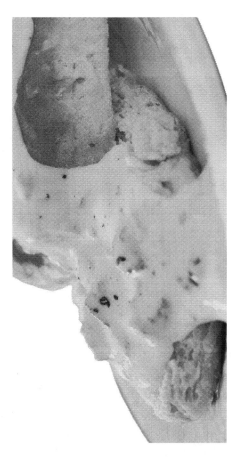

- 1 package (12 ounces) uncooked ground breakfast sausage
- 1 tablespoon kosher salt
- 2 teaspoons ground black pepper
- 2 tablespoons unsalted butter
- 1/4 cup all-purpose flour
- 3 cups whole milk
- 1 tube (16.3 ounces) refrigerated biscuit dough
- 5 egg

1. Set SEAR/SAUTÉ to (Hi). To begin, press the START/STOP button. Allow for a 3-minute preheat.
2. After 3 minutes of preheating, add the sausage, salt, and pepper to the pot. Allow the meat to brown for 5 minutes, breaking it up with a wooden spoon.
3. After 5 minutes, add the butter and thoroughly melt it, then add the flour and whisk to combine. After then, Cook for 2 minutes, then whisk in the milk. Bring to a simmer, then boil for 5 minutes, or until thickened.
4. Separate the biscuit dough rounds and arrange them equally on top of the gravy.
5. In a small dish, crack one egg. Pour the egg on top of the biscuits. Repeat with the remaining eggs, spreading them equally.
6. Select BAKE, 325°F, and 15 minutes. To begin, press the START/STOP button.
7. Check the eggs for doneness after 10 minutes.
8. Cook for a further 5 minutes, if desired.
9. When the eggs have set and the biscuits have cooked through, the cooking is finished. Allow to cool slightly before serving

BREAKFAST FRITTATA

Prep: 5mins. Cook Time: 12mins. SERVINGS: 6-8

- 2 tablespoons unsalted butter
- 1/4 cup onion, diced
- 1 cup honey ham, shredded or chopped
- 7 eggs, lightly beaten
- 3 tablespoons water
- 1 cup Swiss or Gruyère cheese, shredded or diced

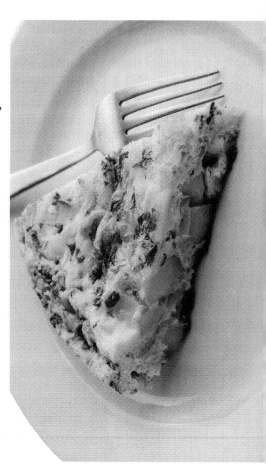

1. Set SEAR/SAUTÉ to 4 (medium-high).
2. To begin, press the START/STOP button. Allow for a 3-minute preheat.
3. After 3 minutes, add the butter and onion to the pot and cook for another minutes, stirring regularly.
4. Cook, stirring periodically, for approximately 3 minutes after adding the onion. Cook for 2 minutes more after adding the ham.
5. Stir in the eggs and cheese using a rubber spatula.
6. Close the crisping cover. Choose BAKE. Set the temperature to 350°F and the timer to 7 minutes.
7. To begin, press the START/STOP button.
8. Allow to cool somewhat after cooking before serving.

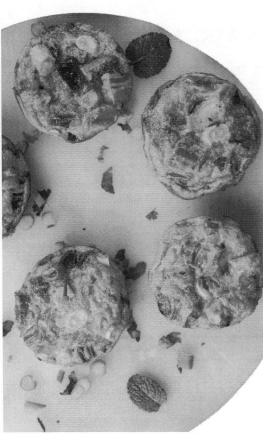

Sous Vide Egg Bites

Prep: 5mins.   Cook Time: 1hour. SERVINGS: 6

- **8 large eggs**
- **1/4 tsp kosher salt**
- **1/4 tsp freshly ground black pepper**
- **1 cup shredded cheese of your choice**
- **3/4 cup chopped green onions**
- **non-stick cooking spray**

1. Spray each mason jar liberally with nonstick oil spray.
2. Fill each mason jar approximately 1/3 full with chopped green onions and cheese (or your preferred additions).
3. Whisk together eggs, salt, and pepper in a large measuring cup.
4. Pour the egg mixture into the jar, leaving approximately 1/2 inch at the top. (If you don't pour enough mixture into the jar, the mason jars may float in the water bath.)
5. "Fingertip tight" shut the lid. (You can simply open it with two fingers).
6. Fill the pot halfway with water and set the sous vide to 172°F (73°C) (place a trivet mat underneath the pot to protect your countertop!)
7. Place the mason jars in the water before it becomes hot. Set the timer for one hour.
8. When the timer goes off, take the jars from the water and set them aside to cool for approximately 10 minutes.
9. To loosen, run a knife along the jar's edges. Remove from the jars and serve warm.

Sous Vide Poached Eggs

Prep: 5mins.   Cook Time: 14mins. SERVINGS: 12

- **12 large eggs**
- **salt and pepper for serving**
- **optional chopped parsley**

1. Fill the pot with water. Set the sous vide to 167°F (75°C).
2. Gently drop the eggs into the bottom of the container using the tongs.
3. Cook for 14 minutes sous vide.
4. When the timer goes off, take the eggs and immerse them in an ice bath. (You may also run them under cold tap water for 1 minute).
5. Tap the egg's larger end on the counter and slowly crack it. Remove the shell from each egg and place it in a separate dish. (You can also drizzle them immediately over toast and salad.)
6. Season with salt, pepper, and optional chopped parsley. Serve and enjoy!

BANANA BREAD

- **2 cups all-purpose flour**
- **1 teaspoon baking soda**
- **1/4 teaspoon kosher salt**
- **1 stick (1/2 cup) butter, softened**
- **3/4 cup dark brown sugar**
- **2 eggs, beaten**
- **3 medium ripe bananas, mashed**

1. Close lid. Preheat the unit by choosing BAKE, 325°F, and 5 minutes. To begin, press the START/STOP button.
2. Meanwhile, whisk together the flour, baking soda, and salt in a mixing dish.
3. In a separate dish, cream together the butter and brown sugar. Stir in the eggs and bananas.
4. Slowly add the dry ingredients to the wet mixture, stirring until just mixed.
5. Grease the Ninja pan (or an 8-inch baking pan) and pour the batter into it.
6. Place the pan in the cooking pot after the unit has heated. Close lid. Select
7. BAKE, 325°F, and 40 minutes. To begin, press the START/STOP button.
8. When the cooking is finished, take the pan from the pot and lay it on a cooling rack. After then, Allow the bread to cool for 30 minutes before serving.

CHOCOLATE CHIP COOKIE

- **1 cup + 2 tablespoons all-purpose flour**
- **1/2 teaspoon baking soda**
- **1/2 teaspoon kosher salt**
- **1 stick (1/2 cup) unsalted butter,**
- **softened, plus more for greasing**
- **6 tablespoons granulated sugar**
- **6 tablespoons packed brown sugar**
- **1/2 teaspoon vanilla extract**
- **1 large egg**
- **1 cup semi-sweet chocolate chips**
- **1/2 cup chopped walnuts, pecans, or almonds, if desired**

1. Close lid. Preheat the unit by choosing BAKE, 325°F, and 5 minutes. To begin, press the START/STOP button.
2. While the oven is heating up, whisk together the flour, baking soda, and salt in a mixing dish.
3. In a separate mixing bowl, cream together the butter, sugars, and vanilla until creamy. Then, Add the egg and beat until smooth and well combined.
4. Slowly add the dry ingredients to the egg mixture, approximately 1/3 at a time. Scrape down the edges with a rubber spatula to ensure that all of the dry ingredients are combined. If you over-mix the dough, the cookie will become thick when cooked.
5. Fold the chocolate chips and nuts into the cookie dough until equally distributed.
6. Grease the Ninja pan (or an 8-inch baking pan) generously.
7. Spread the cookie batter evenly in the pan.
8. Place the pan in the cooking pot after the unit has heated. Close lid. Select BAKE, 325°F, and 23 minutes. To begin, press the START/STOP button.
9. Allow the cookie to cool for 5 minutes after cooking. After then, serve warm with your preferred toppings.

EASY BREAD

- **500 g Strong White Flour**
- **7 g Fast-action Yeast (one sachet)**
- **2 tsp Salt**
- **3 tbsp Butter/Margarine/Oil (whichever you prefer)**
- **300 ml Warm Water**

1. Combine the flour, yeast, and salt in a large mixing bowl.
2. Make a well in the center of the mixture and add the butter/margarine/oil and warm water. Mix to incorporate, adding a little more water if necessary, and using your hands to form a soft, lumpy, somewhat sticky dough.
3. Turn the dough out onto a floured surface and knead for 10 minutes, or until it is smooth and elastic.
4. Cover the dough in the pot. Set the dial to PROOF, the timer to 60 minutes, and the temperature to 95°F. To start proof press START/STOP.
5. Line a baking sheet with greaseproof paper and put aside. Knock back the dough (by gently knocking the air out of the dough and pulling it back on itself) before shaping it into the desired loaf shape.
6. Place the loaf on the prepared baking sheet and let proof for another 45 minutes.
7. Preheat the conventional oven to 250°C.
8. Make a few scores on the top of your bread with a sharp knife before baking. Bake for 25-30 minutes, or until golden brown and the bread sounds hollow when tapped beneath.
9. Allow to cool before serving, or serve warm with lots of butter.

BAKED CHICKEN BREASTS

- **4 boneless skinless chicken breasts, pounded to even thickness**
- **1 tablespoon melted butter or olive oil**
- **1 teaspoon kosher salt**
- **1/2 teaspoon freshly-ground black pepper**
- **1/2 teaspoon garlic powder**
- **1/2 teaspoon smoked paprika**

1. Marinate the chicken. (Check the label on your chicken breasts. If they have previously been pre-brined in a sodium solution, please omit this step.) Fill a large mixing bowl with 1 quart warm water and 1/4 cup kosher salt. After then, Stir until most of the salt is absorbed. Allow the chicken breasts to brine in the mixture for 15 minutes, or cover and chill for up to 6 hours. Remove the chicken breasts from the brine, rinse with cold water, and pat dry with paper towels.
2. Heat the oven. Preheat the conventional oven to 450°F.
3. Season the chicken. Place the chicken breasts in a single layer in the pot. Brush both sides equally with melted butter or olive oil (rotating once). In a separate small bowl, stir together the salt, pepper, garlic powder, and paprika. Sprinkle the seasoning mixture equally over the chicken on both sides.
4. Next, Bake for 15-18 minutes, or until the chicken is cooked through and no longer pink. (If you want the chicken to be a little more browned and crispier on top, set the broiler on high for the last 3-5 minutes of cooking time and then, broil the chicken until it is cooked through and golden on top. Keep an eye on the chicken to ensure it does not overcook or burn.)
5. Rest the chicken. When the chicken is done, take it from the oven, transfer it to a clean plate, and tent it loosely with aluminum foil. Lastly, Allow the chicken to rest for at least 5-10 minutes.
6. Serve hot and enjoy

Baked Potato

Prep: 2mins.   Cook Time: 50mins. SERVINGS: 1

- 1 medium-to-large Russet potato, scrubbed clean of any dirt
- 1–2 teaspoons melted butter (or olive oil)
- pinch of coarse Kosher salt
- pinch of freshly-cracked black pepper

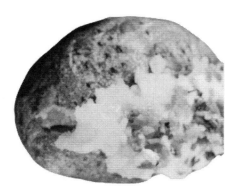

1. Preheat the conventional oven to 450°F. Line the pot with parchment paper.
2. Poke the potato at least ten times on both sides with a dinner fork or a tiny paring knife. Then, Place the potato on the prepared baking sheet.
3. Bake for 25 minutes. Remove the pot from the oven.
4. Brush the outside of the potato with melted butter or olive oil using a pastry brush until it is well covered on both sides. Return the potato to the baking sheet, reverse-side-up, to allow it to cook equally on both sides.
5. Bake for a further 20 minutes. Squeeze the potato gently with an oven mitt to check for doneness. Remove the potato from the oven if the insides are tender and under pressure. Otherwise, heat in 5-minute intervals until the potato is tender.
6. Cut the potato. Cut the potato lengthwise midway with a thin paring knife. Then gently squeeze it open.
7. Serve immediately with your preferred toppings.

Baked Fruit Crisp

Prep: 5mins.   Cook Time: 12mins. SERVINGS: 8

- **FOR THE FILLING:**
- 1/2 cup granulated sugar
- 2 tablespoons cornstarch
- 6 cups sliced fresh or thawed frozen fruit, such as peaches, plums, or cherries
- 1 tablespoon freshly squeezed lemon juice

- **FOR THE TOPPING:**
- 1 1/2 cups old-fashioned rolled oats
- 1 cup all-purpose flour
- 1/2 cup packed light brown sugar
- 1/2 teaspoon salt
- 12 tbps (6 ounces) unsalted butter, melted and cooled, plus more for buttering the baking dish

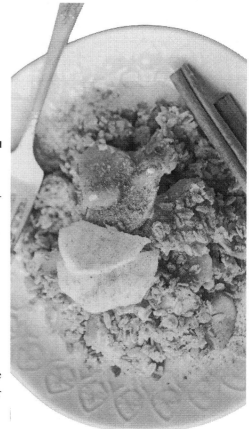

1. Preheat the conventional oven to 450°F. Set aside. Coat the pot with butter.
2. In a medium mixing bowl, whisk together the sugar and cornstarch until lump-free. Toss in the fruit and lemon juice to coat. Transfer to the pot.
3. In a large mixing bowl, toss together the oats, flour, sugar, and salt.
4. Drizzle the butter and vanilla over the oat mixture and toss to incorporate.
5. Set aside or freeze in a zip-top freezer bag for later use.
6. Scatter the crisp topping evenly over the fruit mixture, leaving big clumps intact.
7. Place the pot in the oven and bake for 30 to 35 minutes, or until the fruit juices are bubbling around the sides of the baking dish and the topping is golden and firm to the touch.
8. Then, Allow the crisp to cool for at least 15 minutes before serving.
9. Allow the crisp to fully cool before transporting it to a picnic or party to allow the fruit filling to become firm. Crisps may be stored, covered, and refrigerated, for up to a week. Serve cold, at room temperature, or reheated in a low for 20 minutes.

STEAMED APPLES

Prep: 5mins.   Cook Time: 10mins.

- **5 apples {fuji or gala work great}**
- **1 tsp ground cinnamon**

1. Peel the apples and divide them into bite-sized pieces or cut them into slices.
2. Set the pot to LO steam and add inch of water.
3. Add the apples to the pot.
4. Steam the apples until they are easily pierced with a knife (approximately 4-5 minutes).
5. Drain and stir with cinnamon in a small bowl

STEAMED SPRING ROLLS

Prep: 10mins.   Cook Time: 30mins. SERVINGS: 10

- 12 Pieces Mushrooms
- 12 Chicken (cut lengthwise)
- 12 Fish (cut length wise)
- 12 Crab (cut lengthwise)
- 12 Roots of yam

1. Roll the fish, crab, chicken, and mushroom on a slice of yam root.
2. Make all of the rolls in the same manner.
3. Now steam the rolls for 5 minutes in the pot, then serve

CAULIFLOWER GNOCCHI

Prep: 25mins.   Cook Time: 15mins. SERVINGS: 6

- **1 small head cauliflower,broken into florets**
- **1/3 cup whole-milk ricotta cheese**
- **1 large egg yolk**
- **1 teaspoon salt**
- **3/4 to 1 cup all-purpose flour**
- **1/4 cup butter**
- **Fried sage leaves, optional**

1. Place a steamer rack in the pot over 1 inch of water. Place the cauliflower on a rack. Bring to a boil. Set steam on a LO, cover, and cook until tender, 8-10 minutes. Drain. When the cauliflower is cold enough to

   handle, wrap it in a clean kitchen towel and squeeze it dry.

2. In a food processor, puree the ricotta for 20-30 seconds, or until smooth.

   Add cauliflower and egg yolk till smooth. Add 3/4 cup flour and pulse until the mixture forms a soft dough, adding more flour as required.

   Divide the dough into four equal pieces. Roll each half into 1/2-inch thick

   ropes on a floured surface; cut into 1/2-inch pieces.

3. Then, Bring the water to a boil in the pot. Cook gnocchi in batches for 30-60 seconds, or until they float. Remove with tongs. Choose sear/saute. Melt the butter in the pot. Cook for 3-4 minutes on HI until the gnocchi begins to brown. Garnish with sage, if preferred. Serve immediately.

POULTRY

SOUS VIDE TERIYAKI CHICKEN

Prep: 10mins.   Cook Time: 1hour. SERVINGS: 4

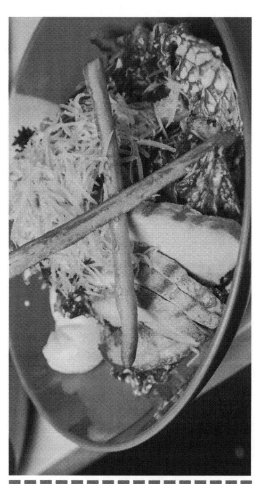

- 1 ½ lb chicken breasts (boneless skinless, fresh or frozen)
- 3 tablespoons sugar
- 1/4 cup soy sauce
- 2 tablespoons rice vinegar
- 2 cloves garlic minced
- 1/2 tablespoon vegetable oil
- 1 tablespoon cornstarch
- 1 tablespoon water

1. Fill the pot with water. Set the sous vide at 149°F (65°C).
2. In a small mixing dish, combine soy sauce, sugar, rice vinegar, chopped garlic, and oil.
3. Place the chicken breasts in a zip-top bag with the sauce.
4. Arrange the breasts in a single layer and then close the bag using the "water displacement" technique: seal all but one corner of the bag and gently immerse it in cold water. Make sure that everything underneath the zip-line is submerged in water. Then close the remaining part of the bag.
5. After then, cook for 1 hour in the sous vide water. (Ensure that the meat is completely immersed while the bag's seams are above water.)
6. When the timer goes off, take the chicken out of the bag. Don't throw away the juices
7. Dry the chicken with paper towels before cutting it into bite-sized pieces.
8. Set the pot on high and pour in the juices from the bag.
9. Mix cornstarch and water in a small bowl. After then, pour the mixture into the pot.
10. Stir frequently for a few minutes, or until the sauce thickens.
11. Remove from the heat and stir in the chicken pieces. Coat the chicken equally. Serve hot with your favorite sides.

HAWAIIAN CHICKEN

TOTAL TIME: 40 minutes + marinating. Serves: 4

- 1 pound chicken, cubed
- 1/2 cup prepared teriyaki sauce
- 2 bell peppers, chopped
- 1/2 cup onion, chopped
- 1/2 cup sliced carrots
- 1/2 cup broccoli florets
- 1/4 tsp. red pepper flakes, to taste
- 1/2 cup pineapple chunks
- For serving: cooked rice
- For serving: additional teriyaki sauce
- Optional toppings: sesame seeds, green onions

1. Marinate the chicken in teriyaki sauce for at least 1 hour and up to overnight
2. Preheat the conventional oven to 375°F.
3. Coat the pot with nonstick cooking spray. Then, remove the chicken from the marinade and toss out the leftover marinade.
4. Season the chicken, bell peppers, onion, carrots, and broccoli on a big sheet pan with red pepper flakes.
5. After then, Bake for 20 minutes, then add the pineapple.
6. Bake for 10-12 minutes, or until the chicken is cooked to an internal temperature of 165°F and the veggies are soft.
7. However If desired, sprinkle with sesame seeds and green onions.
8. Serve with rice and more teriyaki sauce, if preferred.

TURKEY BREAST

Prep: 10mins.   Cook Time: 3hrs 15mins. SERVINGS: 4

- **1 (about 6 lb.) bone-in, skin-on turkey breast, room temperature**
- 2 tbsp. packed light brown sugar
- 1 tbsp. chili powder
- 1 tbsp. smoked paprika
- 1 tsp. garlic powder
- Kosher salt
- Freshly ground black pepper
- 1/2 c. low-sodium chicken broth
- 1/4 c. low-sodium soy sauce
- 2 tbsp. honey
- 2 tbsp. freshly chopped parsley

1. Coat the pot with cooking spray. Roll a huge piece of aluminum foil into a rope, then fold the rope into an oval. Place a rack for the turkey in the pot.

2. In a small mixing bowl, combine brown sugar, chili powder, paprika, and garlic powder. Pat the turkey dry with paper towels and season well with salt and pepper. Spread the sugar mixture all over the turkey, then set it in the pot, breast side up.

3. Pour chicken stock, soy sauce, and honey into the bottom of the pot.

4. Select a slow cooker and Cook on low for 3 to 4 hours, or until a thermometer inserted into the thickest portion of the breast registers 165°.

5. Turn on the broiler. Transfer the turkey to a rimmed baking sheet and broil for 3 to 4 minutes, or until the skin is crispy and golden. Then, Allow to rest for 15 minutes before slicing.

6. Garnish with parsley and serve.

CHICKEN AND CASHEW STEAMED BUNS

Prep: 30 min. + resting Cook: 20 min. 1 dozen

- 1/2 pound ground chicken
- 3 green onions, finely chopped
- 2 tablespoons finely chopped cashews
- 1 tablespoon large egg white
- 1-1/2 teaspoons brown sugar
- 1 teaspoon minced fresh gingerroot
- 1/4 teaspoon sesame oil
- 1 pound fresh or frozen pizza dough, thawed
- 1 cup thinly sliced cabbage
- Hoisin sauce, optional
- 1/4 teaspoon sesame oil

1. In a small mixing bowl, combine the first 8 ingredients until they form a paste. Roll the dough out into a 12x9-inch rectangle on a lightly floured board. Cut into twelve 3-inch squares. Divide the chicken mixture among the squares. Bring four corners of the dough together and twist and pinch to seal. Allow for a 15-minute rest period.

2. Place a steamer rack over 1 inch of water in the pot. Line the rack with cabbage. Place four buns on the rack in batches. Bring the water to a boil. Steam the LO cover for 18-20 minutes, or until a thermometer registers 165°. Carefully remove the cover to prevent pouring moisture onto the buns. If desired, top with hoisin sauce.

21

CHIVE BUTTER SAUCE AND BRAISED CHICKEN WITH POTATOES

Prep:15mins.   Cook Time:50mins. SERVINGS: 6

- 1 pound baby Yukon gold potatoes
- 2 tablespoons extra-virgin olive oil
- 8 bone-in, skin-on, chicken thighs, fat trimmed (about 3 pounds)
- 2 teaspoons kosher salt,
- plus more to taste
- 2 large shallots,
- cut into ½-inch slices
- 6 cloves garlic, thinly sliced
- ⅔ cup chicken stock
- 1 lemon, sliced
- 1½ teaspoons lemon juice, from 1 lemon
- 4 tablespoons salted butter, cold

- For serving
- Freshly cracked black pepper,
- 2 tablespoons finely chopped fresh chives
- Cooked rice, (optional)
- Couscous, (optional)

1. Preheat the conventional oven to 400°F.
2. Bring the pot of water to a boil and salt it. Add the potatoes and Cook for 5 minutes, or until the potatoes are fork tender, then drain. Once the potatoes have cooled enough to touch, cut them in halves.
3. Meanwhile, in the pot, choose sear/saute and heat the olive oil on high. After then, Season the chicken all over with salt.
4. Working in batches, put the chicken in the pot, skin side down, and cook until the skin is browned, approximately 4-5 minutes. Cook until the chicken is browned on the other side, approximately 3 minutes longer. Transfer the chicken to a plate. Add as many potatoes as will fit in the pot, cut sides down, and boil until gently browned about 1-2 minutes. Place the potatoes on a plate alongside the chicken. Repeat until all of the potatoes are browned.
5. Cook, stirring occasionally, until the shallots are gently browned, 2 to 3 minutes. Cook until the garlic is aromatic, roughly 1 minute. Bring to a simmer with the chicken stock. Add the chicken to the broth, skin side up. Nestle the potatoes and top with the lemon slices.
6. Cook until the potatoes are cooked, approximately 35 minutes, in the conventional oven. Transfer the chicken to a plate.
7. Stir in the lemon juice and butter until combined, then season with salt to taste. Return the chicken to the sauce and sprinkle with pepper and chives.
8. Serve family style with cooked rice or couscous.

22

BEER BRAISED CHICKEN

- 2 tablespoons vegetable oil
- 5 chicken thighs , bone in and skin on
- 1 teaspoon Kosher salt
- 1/2 teaspoon coarse ground black pepper
- 1 yellow onion , sliced

- 8 ounces crimini mushrooms sliced
- 12 ounces beer
- 1 cup chicken broth
- 1 teaspoon spicy brown mustard
- 1 teaspoon dried thyme

1. Preheat the conventional oven to 375°F. Select sear/saute on HI and add vegetable oil pot.
2. Season the chicken with salt and pepper and place it in the pot skin side down.
3. Sear the chicken for 3-4 minutes until browned, then turn over and cook for another 3-4 minutes.
4. Switch to LO, add the onions, and cook for 4-5 minutes, or until transparent.
5. Place the chicken in the the pot with the onions and mushrooms.
6. Pour the beer, broth, spicy brown mustard, and dried thyme over the chicken.
7. Bake for 50-60 minutes, uncovered, until the sauce has thickened and the chicken is browned and crispy

SLOW COOKER CHICKEN TIKKA MASALA

- 4 boneless skinless chicken breasts cut into 1 inch pieces
- 1 small onion chopped
- 3 cloves garlic minced
- 2 Tablespoons fresh ginger grated
- 1 29 oz can tomato puree
- 1½ cups plain Greek yogurt
- 2 Tablespoons olive oil
- 2 Tablespoons Garam Masala
- 1 Tablespoon cumin

- ½ Tablespoon paprika
- 2 teaspoon salt
- ¾ teaspoon cinnamon
- ¾ tsp black pepper
- 1 tsp cayenne pepper
- 2 bay leaves
- 1 cup heavy cream
- ½ Tablespoon cornstarch cilantro chopped for garnish

1. Choose slow cook. Combine onion, garlic, ginger, tomato puree, Greek yogurt, olive oil, cayenne pepper, garam masala, black pepper, cumin, paprika, salt, and cinnamon.

2. Toss in the chicken pieces to coat with the sauce. Mix in the bay leaves. Cook on low high for 3 hours.

3. During the final 20 minutes of cooking, stir together cornstarch and heavy cream. Continue to simmer for another 20 minutes after adding to the sauce.

4. Serve over rice.

23

SLOW-COOKER GARLIC-PARMESAN CHICKEN

Prep: 4mins.   Cook Time: 4hrs 15mins. SERVINGS: 4

- 3 tbsp. extra-virgin olive oil, divided
- 2 lb. bone-in, skin-on chicken thighs
- Kosher salt
- Freshly ground black pepper
- 1 lb. baby red potatoes, quartered
- 2 tbsp. butter, softened
- 5 cloves garlic, chopped
- 2 tbsp. fresh thyme
- Freshly chopped parsley

1. Heat 1 tablespoon oil in the pot. Select saute/sear on low. Season the chicken with salt and pepper and sear until brown, about 3 minutes on each side.
2. Toss potatoes with the remaining 2 tablespoons of oil, butter, garlic, thyme, parsley, and Parmesan, and season liberally with salt and pepper. Cook for 4 hours on high, or until potatoes are soft and chicken is thoroughly cooked.
3. Before serving, sprinkle with Parmesan.

BROWN SUGAR BBQ CHICKEN

Prep: 4mins.   Cook Time: 4hrs 15mins. SERVINGS: 6

- 2 lb. boneless skinless chicken breasts
- 1 c. barbecue sauce, plus more for serving
- 1/2 c. packed light or brown sugar
- 1/4 c. bourbon
- 1/4 c. Italian dressing
- 2 tsp. garlic powder
- 1 tsp. paprika
- Kosher salt
- Freshly ground black pepper
- 6 potato buns
- Coleslaw, for serving

1. Combine the chicken breasts, barbecue sauce, brown sugar, bourbon, Italian dressing, garlic powder, and paprika in the pot. Season with salt and pepper.
2. Toss until evenly covered, then cover and cook on high for 4 hours or low for 6 hours.
3. Serve shredded chicken on buns with a sprinkle of barbecue sauce and a tablespoon of coleslaw.

24

SLOW-COOKER CREAMY LEMON HERB CHICKEN

- 1 1/2 lb. skinless, boneless chicken breasts (about 4)
- Kosher salt
- Freshly ground black pepper
- 4 tbsp. (1/2 stick) unsalted butter
- 1 1/2 c. low-sodium chicken stock
- 1 shallot, finely chopped
- 4 cloves garlic, finely chopped
- 3 thyme sprigs
- 1 rosemary sprig
- 2 tbsp. water
- 2 tsp. cornstarch
- 1/2 c. heavy cream
- 2 tsp. finely grated lemon zest
- 2 tbsp. fresh lemon juice
- Chopped fresh parsley, for serving

1. Set sear/sauté on LO. Melt butter and season the chicken with 2 teaspoons salt and 1/2 teaspoon pepper. Arrange the chicken in an equal layer in the pot and cook, rotating once, until golden brown, 2 to 3 minutes on each side.
2. Put the chicken in the pot. Pour the stock into the pot, scraping away any stuck-on pieces, and then pour over the chicken.
3. Add the shallot, garlic, thyme, and rosemary to the pot. Cover and set slow cook to high for 4 hours or low for 6 hours, or until chicken is extremely soft. Remove the herb stems.
4. During the final 20 minutes of cooking, mix together the water and cornstarch in a small bowl and pour into the pot. Mix in the cream, lemon zest, and lemon juice. Cook on high or low for approximately 20 minutes, or until the sauce is slightly thickened and warmed through.
5. Divide the chicken and sauce among the dishes. Garnish with parsley if desired.

ASPARAGUS BEEF SAUTE

- 1 pound beef tenderloin or top sirloin steak, cut into 3/4-inch cubes
- 1/2 teaspoon salt
- 1/4 teaspoon pepper
- 1 tablespoon canola oil
- 2 garlic cloves, minced
- 1 green onion, sliced
- 1/4 cup butter, cubed
- 1 pound fresh asparagus, trimmed and cut into 2-inch pieces
- 1/2 pound sliced fresh mushrooms
- 1 tablespoon reduced-sodium soy sauce
- 1-1/2 teaspoons lemon juice
- Hot cooked rice

1. Season beef with salt and pepper. Select saute/sear on low in the possiblecooker, heat the oil, and sauté the beef for 2 minutes. Cook and stir until beef is browned, about 2-3 minutes. Remove from the cooker.
2. Heat butter in the same pot and sauté asparagus and mushrooms until asparagus is crisp-tender. Heat through, stirring to incorporate the beef, soy sauce, and lemon juice. Serve with rice.

25

EASY PEPPER CHICKEN STIR FRY

- For the Marinade
- 4 chicken breasts cut into 1 inch pieces
- 2 tablespoons light soy sauce
- 1 teaspoon garlic minced
- 1 tablespoon toasted sesame oil
- 1 teaspoon ground black pepper

  - For the Stir Fry
  - ¼ cup oyster sauce
  - 2 tablespoons light soy sauce
  - ½ cup water
  - 3 tablespoons cornstarch divided
  - 3 tablespoons vegetable oil divided
  - 1 large onion cut into 1 inch pieces
  - 1 medium green bell pepper cut into 1 inch pieces
  - 1 medium red bell pepper cut into 1 inch pieces
  - 4 cloves garlic finely chopped
  - 1 inch piece ginger finely chopped

  - 2 tablespoon vinegar
  - 1 teaspoon ground black pepper

1. Combine all of the marinade ingredients, including the chicken, and set aside for at least 15 minutes.
2. Set aside the oyster sauce, soy sauce, vinegar, black pepper, half a cup of water, and one tablespoon of cornstarch.
3. Toss the chicken in the remaining two tablespoons of cornstarch once it has marinated.
4. Choose saute/sear on HI. In the pot, heat two teaspoons of oil and add the chicken pieces. Don't overcrowd the pot, and if it's a little more, do it in batches. Cook the chicken pieces for 3 minutes on each side over high heat. Remove the pieces from the pot and put aside.
5. On high heat, add the remaining tablespoon of oil and the onions and bell peppers. Toss them in the pot for a minute or two, or until they brighten in color and begin to cook slightly. Cook for an additional minute after adding the ginger and garlic.
6. Then, Add the chicken pieces and sauce mixture to the pot. Toss everything together and cook for a minute or two, or until the sauce thickens and covers the chicken nicely. Lastly, Serve hot with steamed rice or veggies on the side.

26

VEGETABLES SLIDES

Slow Cooker Vegan Butternut Squash Soup

Prep:10mins.   Cook Time: 6hrs 15mins. SERVINGS:4

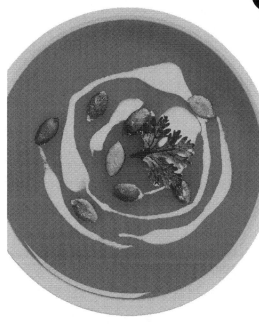

- 1 (13.5-oz.) can full-fat unsweetened coconut milk
- 4 c. low-sodium vegetable stock
- 1 (2-lb.) butternut squash, peeled, seeded, roughly chopped
- 2 large carrots, peeled, roughly chopped
- 2 shallots, peeled, roughly chopped
- 4 cloves garlic
- 1 (2") piece ginger, peeled, minced or grated
- 1 tbsp. red curry paste
- Kosher salt
- Zest and juice of 1 lime
- Chopped fresh cilantro, for serving

1. 1. Set aside 2 tablespoons of the coconut milk for drizzling.
2. Combine the remaining coconut milk, stock, squash, carrots, shallots, garlic, ginger, curry paste, and 1 tablespoon salt in the pot.
3. Select slow cook and simmer on high for 4 hours, or until veggies are extremely tender.
4. Add the lime zest and juice. Blend the soup with an immersion blender until it is completely smooth. (Alternatively, ladle soup into a regular blender and process until smooth, working in batches if required.)
5. Ladle soup into bowls. Drizzle with the reserved coconut milk. Garnish with cilantro if desired.

CHEESY ZUCCHINI SAUTE

Prep: 5mins.   Cook Time: 15mins. SERVINGS: 6

- 1/2 cup chopped onion
- 1/4 cup butter, cubed
- 3 cups coarsely shredded zucchini
- 2 teaspoons minced fresh basil or
- 1/2 teaspoon dried basil
- 1/2 teaspoon salt
- 1/8 teaspoon garlic powder
- 1 cup shredded cheddar cheese
- 1 cup diced fresh tomato
- 2 tablespoons sliced ripe olives

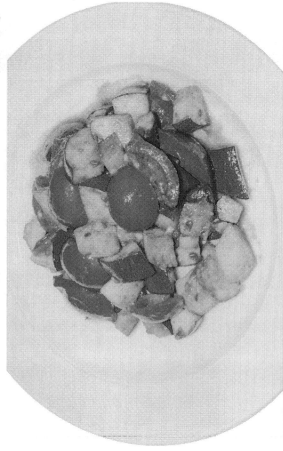

1. In a pot, set to sear/saute on LO to sauté onion in butter until crisp-tender.
2. Mix in the zucchini, basil, salt, and garlic powder. After, Cook and stir for 4-5 minutes or until zucchini is crisp-tender. Then, Sprinkle with the cheese, tomato, and olives.
3. Cook, covered, for 4-5 minutes, or until the cheese is melted. Serve immediately.

THYMED ZUCCHINI SAUTE

Prep: 5mins.   Cook Time: 10mins. SERVINGS: 6

- 1 pound medium zucchini, quartered lengthwise and halved
- 1/4 cup finely chopped onion
- 1/2 vegetable bouillon cube, crushed
- 1 tablespoon olive oil
- 2 tablespoons minced freshparsley
- 1 teaspoon minced fresh thyme or
- 1/4 teaspoon dried thyme

1. Choose saute/sear on low heat oil in a possible cooker. Then, Cook and stir for 4-5 minutes, or until zucchini is crisp-tender. Garnish with herbs if desired.

SAUTEED GARLIC MUSHROOMS

Prep: 5mins.   Cook Time: 10mins. SERVINGS: 6

- 3/4 pound sliced fresh mushrooms
- 2 to 3 teaspoons minced garlic
- 1 tablespoon seasoned bread crumbs
- 1/3 cup butter, cubed

1. In a possible cooker, choose saute/sear on low and sauté the mushrooms, garlic, and bread crumbs in butter until the mushrooms are soft, 3-5 minutes.

29

SOUTHWESTERN SAUTEED CORN

Prep: 5mins.   Cook Time: 10mins. SERVINGS: 6

- 1 tablespoon butter
- 3-1/3 cups fresh corn or
- 1 package (16 ounces) frozen corn
- 1 plum tomato, chopped
- 1 tablespoon lime juice
- 1/2 teaspoon salt
- 1/2 teaspoon ground cumin
- 1/3 cup minced fresh cilantro

1. In a possible cooker, choose saute/sear on low and melt butter. Cook and stir corn for 3-5 minutes, or until soft. Mix in the tomato, lime juice, salt, and cumin. Cook for 3-4 minutes. Then, Remove the lid and add the cilantro.

SAUTEED SQUASH WITH TOMATOES & ONIONS

Prep: 5mins.   Cook Time: 10mins. SERVINGS: 8

- 2 tablespoons olive oil
- 1 medium onion, finely chopped
- 4 medium zucchini, chopped
- 2 large tomatoes, finely chopped
- 1 teaspoon salt
- 1/4 teaspoon pepper

1. In a possible cooker, choose saute/sear on low, heat oil, then Cook and stir until the onion is soft, 2-4 minutes. Cook and stir for 3 minutes.
2. Cook and mix in the tomatoes, salt, and pepper until the squash is soft, about 4-6 minutes. Serve with a slotted spoon.

30

SAUTEED ORANGE-GLAZED BABY CARROTS

Prep: 5mins. Cook Time: 25mins. SERVINGS: 4

- **1 pound fresh baby carrots**
- **3 tablespoons butter**
- **3 tablespoons thawed orange juice concentrate**
- **1/4 teaspoon dried thyme**
- **1/4 teaspoon paprika**
- **1/4 teaspoon ground cumin**
- **1/8 teaspoon salt**
- **1/8 teaspoon pepper**

1. Select saute/sear on low in the possible cooker and sauté carrots in butter for 8 minutes. Cook for 2 minutes more, then cover and simmer for 8-10 minutes, or until carrots are soft.

SAUTEED RADISHES WITH GREEN BEANS

Prep: 5mins. Cook Time: 15mins. SERVINGS: 4

- **1 tablespoon butter**
- **1/2 pound fresh green or wax beans, trimmed**
- **1 cup thinly sliced radishes**
- **1/2 teaspoon sugar**
- **1/4 teaspoon salt**
- **2 tablespoons pine nuts, toasted**

1. In the possible cooker, Sauté/sear on low heat, melt butter, then Cook and stir for 3-4 minutes, or until the beans are crisp-tender.
2. Cook for another 2-3 minutes, or until vegetables are soft, stirring periodically. Stir in the sugar and salt, then top with the nuts.

31

BALSAMIC ZUCCHINI SAUTE

Prep: 5mins.   Cook Time: 15mins. SERVINGS: 4

- 1 tablespoon olive oil
- 3 medium zucchini, cut into thin slices
- 1/2 cup chopped sweet onion
- 1/2 teaspoon salt
- 1/2 teaspoon dried rosemary, crushed
- 1/4 teaspoon pepper
- 2 tablespoons balsamic vinegar
- 1/3 cup crumbled feta cheese

1. In the possible cooker, Select saute/sear on low, heat oil, and sauté zucchini and onion until crisp-tender, 6-8 minutes. Season with salt and pepper to taste. Cook and stir for 2 minutes after adding vinegar. Top with cheese

---

LEMON-LIME SALMON WITH VEGGIE SAUTE

Prep: 5mins.   Cook Time: 25mins. SERVINGS: 6

- 6 salmon fillets (4 ounces each)
- 1/2 cup lemon juice
- 1/2 cup lime juice
- 1 teaspoon seafood seasoning
- 1/4 teaspoon salt
- 2 medium sweet red peppers, sliced
- 2 medium sweet yellow peppers, sliced
- 1 large red onion, halved and sliced
- 2 teaspoons olive oil
- 1 package (10 ounces) frozen corn, thawed
- 2 cups baby portobello mushrooms, halved
- 2 cups cut fresh asparagus (1-inch pieces)
- 2 tablespoons minced fresh tarragon or
- 2 teaspoons dried tarragon

1. Place the salmon in a 13x9-inch baking dish and drizzle with lemon and lime juices. Season with salt and seafood seasoning to taste. Bake uncovered at 325° for 10 minutes, or until fish flakes effortlessly with a fork.
2. Meanwhile, in the possible cooker, choose to saute/sear on low covered with cooking spray, and sauté peppers and onion in oil for 3 minutes.
3. Cook and stir for 3-4 minutes more, or until the corn, mushrooms, and asparagus are tender. Stir in the tarragon. Serve with salmon.

SICILIAN STEAMED LEEKS

Prep: 5mins.   Cook Time: 15mins. SERVINGS: 4

- **6 medium leeks (white portion only),**
- **halved lengthwise, cleaned**
- **1 large tomato, chopped**
- **1 small navel orange, peeled,**
- **sectioned and chopped**
- **2 tablespoons minced fresh parsley**
- **2 tablespoons sliced Greek olives**
- **1 teaspoon capers, drained**
- **1 teaspoon red wine vinegar**
- **1 teaspoon olive oil**
- **1/2 teaspoon grated orange zest**
- **1/2 teaspoon pepper**
- **Crumbled feta cheese**

1. Place the steamer rack over 1 inch of water in the pot. Place the leeks in the basket. Bring the water to a boil. Set steam to low heat and steam for 8-10 minutes, covered. Meanwhile, mix the following 9 ingredients.
2. Transfer the leeks to a serving plate. Top with tomato mixture and cheese.

VEGAN CASHEW CREAM OF BROCCOLI SOUP

Prep: 20mins.   Cook Time: 30mins. SERVINGS: 8

- 1 bunch broccoli, cut into florets
- 5 cups water, divided
- 1/2 cup raw cashews
- 3 tablespoons vegan butter-style sticks, such as Earth Balance
- 1 medium onion, chopped
- 1 tablespoon minced fresh sage
- 1 tablespoon minced fresh thyme
- 1 teaspoon garlic powder
- 1/2 teaspoon onion powder
- 2 medium Yukon Gold potatoes, peeled and cut into 1-inch pieces
- 1 bay leaf
- 4-1/2 teaspoons no chicken vegetable base or vegetable base
- 1 tablespoon nutritional yeast
- 1/2 teaspoon salt
- 1/4 teaspoon pepper

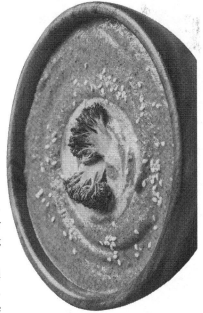

1. Place a steamer rack over 1 inch of water in the pot. Arrange broccoli on a rack. Bring the water to a boil. Set to steam over low heat, covered, for 5-6 minutes, or until just tender. Allow the broccoli to cool before chopping roughly and setting aside.
2. In a blender or food processor, combine 1 cup water and the cashews; cover and process until smooth. Set aside. Set sous vide on high in a pot to melt vegan butter. Cook and stir for 3-4 minutes, or until the onion is just soft. Cook for 1 minute further after adding the sage, thyme, garlic powder, and onion powder. Add the potatoes, bay leaf, vegetable base, and the remaining 4 cups of water.
3. Bring to a boil; cook on low heat for 10-12 minutes, or until potatoes are cooked. Then stir in the nutritional yeast, salt, pepper, cashew mixture, and broccoli. Heat all the way through. Lastly, Remove the bay leaf and set aside.

33

FIDDLEHEADS

- **1 pound fiddleheads, trimmed**
- **1/4 cup butter**
- **2 garlic cloves, minced**
- **2 tablespoons lemon juice**
- **1/2 teaspoon salt**
- **1/4 teaspoon pepper**

1. Place a steamer rack in the pot over 1 inch of water. Place the fiddleheads on the rack. Bring the water to a boil. On a LO, cover, and steam until tender, 10-12 minutes.
2. Set the pot to sear/sauté on high heat and add the fiddleheads. Cook and stir for 5-8 minutes, or until the edges start to brown. Then, Cook for 1 minute after adding the garlic. After then, Mix in the lemon juice, salt, and pepper

STEAMED ARTICHOKE

- **4 medium artichokes (about 12 ounces each)**
- **1 Lemon, halved crosswise**
- **Coarse salt**
- **Easy Hollandaise**
- **Butter, melted (optional)**

1. Take off the tough outer leaves. After then, Cut off the top ⅓ of the artichoke using a serrated knife. With kitchen shears, snip any remaining sharp or prickly points.
2. Trim the stem so that the artichoke stands upright.
3. To avoid discolouration, rub the cut surface with lemon. Repeat with the remaining artichokes and lemon.
4. Set in the pot with adequate water. Next, Squeeze lemon juice into water and add 1 tablespoon salt; bring to a boil. Place artichokes in the pot, stem side up.
5. Cover the pot and steam for 25 to 35 minutes, or until the heart is soft when pierced with the tip of a paring knife and the inner leaves easily come out; add extra water to the pot if required.
6. Serve warm or at room temperature with Easy Hollandaise or melted butter, if preferred.

BEEF, PORK AND LAMB

SLOW-COOKER PULLED PORK

Prep: 10mins.   Cook Time: 6hours. SERVINGS: 8.

- 1 onion, finely chopped
- 3/4 c. ketchup
- 3 tbsp. tomato paste
- 1/4 c. apple cider vinegar
- 1 tsp. paprika
- 1 tsp. garlic powder
- 1 tsp. mustard powder
- 1 tsp. cumin

- 1 (3- to 4-lb.) pork shoulder,
- (trimmed of excess fat)
- Kosher salt
- Freshly ground black pepper
- Coleslaw, for serving
- Buns, for serving

1. select to slow cook, combine the onion, ketchup, tomato paste, apple cider vinegar, and spices. Season the pork shoulder all over with salt and pepper, then add it to the pot and top with the ketchup mixture. Cook until extremely soft (the meat should break apart easily with a fork!) on HIGH for 5 to 6 hours or LOW for 8 to 10 hours.
2. Transfer pork to a bowl. Toss with the pot juices and shred with two forks. Serve on buns with coleslaw.

SOUS VIDE PORK LOIN ROAST

Prep: 10mins.   Cook Time: 3hours. SERVINGS: 6

- 3 pounds pork loin roast boneless
- 1 tablespoon olive oil Dry Rub
- 1 teaspoon kosher salt
- 1 teaspoon ground black pepper
- 1 teaspoon paprika or smoked paprika
- 1 tablespoon garlic powder
- fresh rosemary sprigs

1. Set the Sous Vide at 140°F (60°C).
2. Combine garlic powder, paprika, salt, and pepper.
3. On both sides, rub the pork loin with 1/2 tablespoon oil and the seasoning.
4. Then, Place the seasoned roast in a zip-lock bag (or vacuum-sealer). If you're using a zip-loc bag, utilize the water displacement approach to seal it.
5. Cook for 3 hours in heated water. When the timer goes off, take the bag from the water.
6. Remove the roast from the bag and dry off with paper towels. Add the remaining oil to the heated pot and sear/saute for approximately 1-2 minutes on each side, just to caramelize the outside. Then If necessary, season with more salt and pepper. Slice against the grain and serve.

SANTA MARIA STYLE TRI TIP SOUS VIDE

- **2 ½ pounds tri-tip roast**
- **(It's sometimes called triangle steak or bottom sirloin cut)**
- **1 tablespoon olive oil**
- **Santa Maria Rub**
- **3/4 tablespoon garlic powder**
- **3/4 tablespoon onion powder**
- **1/2 teaspoon cayenne**
- **1 tablespoon dried oregano**
- **1 teaspoon minced rosemary or**
- **dry rosemary**
- **1/2 tablespoon kosher salt**
- **1/2 tablespoon ground black pepper**
- **dry sage leaf optional**

1. Preheat the pot water by adding water to the pot, then set the Sous Vide to 133°F (56°C).
2. Trim away any extra fat from the tri-tip.
3. In a small bowl, combine garlic powder, onion powder, cayenne pepper, dried oregano, rosemary, salt, and pepper.
4. Rub half of the seasoning over the steak.
5. Place the seasoned tri-tip in a large vacuum bag or zip-top bag, along with the optional bay leaf.

6. If you use a zip-loc bag, seal it using the "water displacement" technique: Seal all but one corner of the bag and gently immerse it in cold water. Make sure that everything underneath the zip-line is submerged in water. Then close the remaining part of the bag. (If your tri-tip is too large for one bag, split it into two pieces and use two bags.)
7. When the water has reached the desired temperature, drop the bag into the water bath. Make sure the meat is completely immersed in water, with the bag seams above the water.
8. Sous vide for 2 hours.
9. When the timer goes off, take the tri tip from the bag and let it aside to cool somewhat.
10. With paper towels, pat dry.
11. Rub the remaining seasoning over the sous vide cooked tri-tip.
12. Set the pot to sear/saute on high and add the olive oil. Cook for 1 minute on each side until the tri-tip is well browned.
13. Serve the tri-tip thinly sliced across the grain with potatoes and vegetables.

37

SOUS VIDE RIBEYE STEAK

Prep: 5mins.   Cook Time: 1hour. SERVINGS: 4

- **2 ribeye steaks 1 ½-inch thick**
- **kosher salt to taste**
- **ground black pepper to taste**
- **1 tablespoon olive oil divided**
- **2 tablespoons butter**
- **fresh rosemary optional**

1. Fill the pot with water and set the Sous Vide to 135°F (57°C).
2. Rub 1/2 tablespoon oil on both sides of the steak. Season with salt and pepper.
3. Set the seasoned ribeye in a zip-top bag, then close all but one corner of the bag and gently set it in the pot of cold water. Make sure that everything below the zip line is submerged in water. Then close the remaining part of the bag.
4. Put the bag in the pot of water. Assure that the steak is completely immersed while the bag's seams are above the water.
5. When the timer goes off, take the bag from the water and place it in an ice bath or refrigerator. After then, Allow it to cool for 10 minutes.
6. Remove the steak from the zip-top bag and pat it dry with paper towels.
7. After then if desired, season with more salt and pepper.
8. Set the pot to sear/sauté on high. Once the remaining oil and butter are heated, add everything. When the butter has melted, add the steak and optional rosemary. Sear for 1-2 minutes on each side, or until beautifully browned.
9. Serve with potatoes and vegetables.

38

SOUS VIDE CARNITAS

Prep: 10mins.   Cook Time: 20hours. SERVINGS: 8

- 4-5 pounds pork shoulder or
- pork butt (bone-in or boneless)
- 4 cloves garlic smashed
- 2 teaspoons kosher salt (plus more for serving)
- 1 teaspoon ground black pepper
- 1 tablespoon ground cumin
- 1/2 teaspoon paprika
- 1 teaspoon dried oregano
- 1 lime juiced
- 1 orange juiced
- 3/4 cup beer or chicken stock
- Toppings:
- chopped onions
- cilantro
- sour cream
- lime wedges

1. Remove the extra fat from the pork.
2. In a small bowl, combine salt, pepper, cumin, paprika, crushed garlic, and dried oregano. Rub dry spice all over the pork.
3. In a separate small dish, mix the lime juice, orange juice, and beer together.
4. Fill the pot with water and set the Sous Vide to 160°F (71°C).
5. Place the seasoned pork and fluids in a large vacuum bag or zip-lock bag. If you use zip-lock bags, seal them using the "water displacement" technique: Seal all but one corner of the bag and carefully immerse it in the water bath. Make sure that everything below the zip line is submerged in water. Then close the remaining part of the bag. (If your pork is too large for one bag, split it into two pieces and use two bags.)
6. When the water has reached the desired temperature, drop the bags into the water bath. Make sure the meat is completely immersed in water, with the bag seams above the water.
7. Cook for 18 hours, covered with aluminum foil. This will reduce water evaporation.
8. When the timer goes off, take the bag from the water (but do not discard the juices in the bag).
9. Then, Transfer the pork to a baking sheet and shred it with two forks. Toss the top of the pork with 1 cup of juice from the bag. (Taste the pork and season with more salt if desired.)
10. Choose sear/sauté to boil the pork for 5-10 minutes on high, or until the edges have browned and turned crispy.
11. Remove the baking sheet from the pot, drip extra liquids over the pork and toss to incorporate.
12. Serve heated in tacos or burritos with fresh cilantro and onions.

SLOW-COOKER SHORT RIBS

Prep: 25mins.   Cook Time: 5hours. SERVINGS: 5

- 2 tbsp. vegetable oil
- 5 lb. bone-in beef short ribs,
- cut crosswise into 2-inch pieces
- Kosher salt
- Freshly ground black pepper
- 1/2 c. low-sodium soy sauce
- 1/2 c. water
- 1/4 c. packed light brown sugar
- 1/4 c. rice vinegar
- 2 tsp. sesame oil
- 1 tsp. crush red pepper flakes (optional)
- 3 Carrots, medium, peeled and chopped into thirds
- 1 yellow onion, large,
- sliced into 1/2 inch wedges
- 5 cloves garlic, crushed
- 1 1/2 inch piece ginger, thinly sliced
- For serving
- Toasted sesame seeds,
- 2 green onions, thinly sliced,
- Cooked short grain white rice,

1. Season the short ribs with salt & pepper. On a LO, choose sauté/sear, Heat the oil in a pot. Brown short ribs on both sides in two batches approximately 8 minutes for each batch. Then Place the short ribs in the pot and drain out all except 3 tablespoons of the drippings.

2. Meanwhile, combine soy sauce, water, brown sugar, rice vinegar, sesame oil, and red pepper flakes in a mixing bowl.

3. Cook, stirring periodically, until carrots and onions are browned. Brown the garlic and ginger for 1 minute longer, until fragrant. Remove from heat and deglaze with the leftover soy sauce mixture, scraping off any brown pieces from the bottom. Pour this mixture into the the pot.

4. Cook on high for 4 to 5 hours, or until the ribs are extremely soft and falling off the bone.

5. Garnish the short ribs with toasted sesame seeds and green onions. Serve the sauce over the rice.

SOUS VIDE LAMB CHOPS

Prep: 5mins.   Cook Time: 2hours. SERVINGS: 6

- **8 lamb chops**
- **(loin chops or rib chops)**
- **1 tablespoon minced garlic (about 3 cloves)**
- **2 teaspoons chopped fresh rosemary**
- **(plus a few more sprigs for searing)**
- **kosher salt to taste**
- **ground black pepper to taste**
- **1 tablespoon lemon juice**
- **2 tablespoons olive oil (divided)**

1. Fill the pot halfway with water and set the sous vide temperature to 135°F/57°C.
2. In a medium mixing bowl, combine garlic, rosemary, lemon juice, 1 tablespoon olive oil, salt, and black pepper.
3. Place the lamb chops in a zip-top bag and coat with the mixture. Then, Make sure they're all in one layer.
4. Seal all but one corner of the bag and carefully immerse it in the water bath. And make sure that everything below the zip line is submerged in water. Then, close the remaining part of the bag. (If you have a vacuum sealer, you may also use it.)
5. Cook for around 2 hours with the bag in the water bath.
6. Then, Remove the bag from the water when the timer goes off. Chill the lamb for approximately 10 minutes before cooking it, or keep it in the fridge for 3-4 days.
7. After then, Remove the lamb from the bag and pat dry with paper towels.
8. Set the sear/sauté function to high. add 1 tablespoon oil. Once it is smoking hot, add the lamb chops and sear for approximately 2 minutes on each side, or until beautifully browned. (If desired, add some rosemary sprigs).
9. Transfer the lamb to a chopping board, cover with foil for 5 minutes, and serve.

ROULADEN

- 2-3 lbs Round Roast
- (have butcher slice thinlylength wise @ ⅛ " thick)
- 8-12 slices bacon , optional
- 1 onion very thinly sliced
- 2 carrots very thinly sliced, julienne
- 2 whole dill pickles thinly sliced,
- 1/2 cup German mustard or dijon
- Salt and Pepper
- toothpicks
- 2 Tablespoons butter or oil, or a combination
- 1 cup water or beef broth

1. Cut the onion, carrot, and pickle into matchstick-style pieces.
2. Spread the thin slices of meat with mustard and sprinkle with salt and pepper.
3. Place the bacon on top (if using), followed by the pickle, carrot, and onion along with the meat. After then, Roll up firmly and secure with toothpicks.
4. Choose sear/saute on a LO, and Preheat the pot. Add the butter or oil.
5. Cook, turning periodically, until browned on both sides. Scrape up any browned parts from the pot and add 1 cup water or beef broth to the pot. Cook on low for 2 hours, covered.
6. Transfer the Rouladen to a plate and bring the juices in the pot to a boil. Thicken with 1 tablespoon of cornstarch dissolved in water. If desired, season the gravy with extra salt, pepper, or beef bouillon granules.
7. Remove the toothpicks from the Rouladen and serve with gravy spooned on top.

BRAISED PORK IN SWEET SOY SAUCE

- 2 pound pork loin
- 2 tablespoon vegetable oil
- 1 tablespoon garlic and ginger paste
- 1 tablespoon olive oil
- 1 tablespoon sesame oil
- ½ cup soy sauce
- 4 tablespoon sugar
- 1½ cup water
- 1 tablespoon chili garlic sauce

1. Select sear/sauté on HI, saute in the pot with the vegetable oil for approximately 3 minutes, or until the pork is no longer pink and begins to brown.
2. Then, Combine the remaining ingredients in a medium mixing bowl. Bring to a boil over the pork. You may believe there is too much water, but it will reduced. Once it's boiling, select braise on low and cook for approximately 30 minutes, stirring regularly, or until there's only about 3 tbsp of sauce left.
3. Garnish with green onions. Serve with noodles or steaming rice.

BRAISED PORK ALL'ARRABBIATA

Prep: 20mins.   Cook Time: 3 ½ hours. SERVINGS: 7 cups

- 2 to 2½ pounds boneless pork shoulder,
- trimmed of more than ¼-inch fat
- Kosher salt and black pepper
- 2 tablespoons extra-virgin olive oil
- 10 garlic cloves, peeled and smashed
- 1½ teaspoons red-pepper flakes
- 3(14-ounce) cans fire-roasted
- crushed or diced tomatoes
- 1 cup red wine
- 5 basil sprigs

1. Season the pork all over with 2 tablespoons salt and 1 teaspoon pepper.
2. 2To begin preheating, turn the dial to SEAR/SAUTÉ, set the temperature to HI, and click START/STOP. Allow the device to warm for 5 minutes. When the preheating is complete, add the olive oil. Sear the pork shoulder on both sides for 8 to 10 minutes.
3. Reduce the LO. Stir in the garlic & red pepper flakes. Mix in the tomatoes, red wine, and basil. Stir to incorporate, season with salt and plenty of black pepper, bring to a boil, and cover with a lid. Set the dial to BRAISE, the temperature to H, the time to 2½ -3 hours, and the START/STOP button to continue cooking until the pork comes apart when poked with a fork.
4. Working directly in the the pot, shred the meat with two forks into long bite-size pieces.
5. Stir the pork into the tomato sauce until it is equally distributed. Ragù may be refrigerated for 3 days or frozen for up to 3 months.

SLOW-COOKER POT ROAST

Prep: 30mins.   Cook Time: 5 hours. SERVINGS: 7

- 3/4 c. low-sodium beef broth
- 2 tbsp. tomato paste
- 2 tbsp. Worcestershire sauce
- 1 tbsp. cornstarch
- 1 lb. small potatoes, scrubbed and halved
- 3 carrots, peeled and cut crosswise into 2" pieces
- 1 medium yellow onion,
- cut into 1/2" wedges
- 4 cloves garlic
- 1 sprig rosemary
- 1 (3.5 lb.) beef chuck roast
- Kosher salt
- Freshly ground black pepper

1. Whisk together broth, tomato paste, Worcestershire sauce, and cornstarch in the bottom of a the pot. Add the potatoes, carrots, onion, garlic, and rosemary.
2. Season the beef with salt and pepper before nestling it into the veggies. Cover and set to slow cook on high for 5 hours, or until the roast is fork-tender.
3. Thinly slice the roast and arrange it on top of the veggies on a platter. Skim fat from any remaining juices in the pot and sprinkle over top. Serve warm.

WINE BRAISED BEEF WITH MUSHROOMS

Prep: 40mins.   Cook Time: 3hours.   SERVINGS: 8

- **5 lbs chuck roast, cut into 3-4" pieces, large fat pieces trimmed**
- **2 Tbsp Extra virgin olive oil**
- **1 Tbsp kosher salt**
- **1 medium sized onion, finely diced**
- **2 large carrots, peeled and finely diced**
- **2 bay leaves**
- **4 garlic cloves, smashed**
- **2 Tbsp tomato paste**
- **3 Tbsp all purpose flour**
- **3 cups light red wine, like a Pinot Noir**
- **1 lb crimini mushrooms, quartered**
- **3 sprigs of fresh thyme**
- **pepper**

1. Preheat the conventional oven to 350°F.
2. Pat dry the meat and liberally salt and pepper all sides.
3. Select saute/sear on a LO in the pot, and heat oil until shimmering. Brown both sides of the meat in small batches. 2 minutes per side. Set the meat aside.
4. Add the onions, carrots, and bay leaves. Cook until the carrots and onions are barely soft, approximately 5 minutes. Then, Cook for another 2 minutes after adding the garlic.

5. Stir in the tomato paste. Then, Stir in the flour until it is incorporated. Stir in the wine slowly, then add the mushrooms.
6. After then, Place the meat in the pot in a single layer. The meat should be slightly above the liquid line. You don't want it completely immersed in the liquid. Bring the dish to a boil, then tuck the thyme between the pieces of meat. Cover and put in a preheated conventional oven. Cook for 2½ -3 hours. When the meat is done, it should easily come apart with a fork.
7. Serve in a small dish over a bed of creamy mashed potatoes and with some hearty veggies.

44

DESSERT, SNACKS & APPETIZERS

MAC AND CHEESE

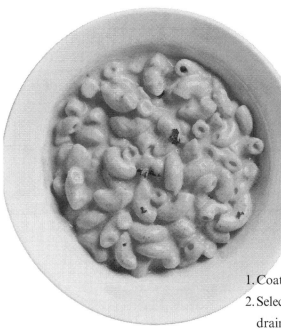

Prep: 20mins.   Cook Time: 2hours. SERVINGS: 8

- **2 cups uncooked elbow macaroni**
- **4 Tablespoons butter**
- **2 ½ cups grated sharp cheddar cheese**
- **½ cup sour cream**
- **10.75 ounces condensed cheddar cheese soup**
- **½ teaspoon salt**
- **1 cup milk**
- **½ teaspoon dry mustard**
- **½ teaspoon black pepper**

1. Coat a possible cooker with nonstick cooking spray.
2. Select low braise, then boil the macaroni in water for six minutes, drain, and rinse with cool water. You don't want to overcook this!
3. Melt butter and cheese together,
4. Slow cook the cheese mixture, sour cream, soup, salt, milk, mustard, and pepper. Add the cooked macaroni. Stir the mixture to combine it.
5. Cook for 2 - 2 ½ hours on low, stirring periodically. Just till it's when hot. If you leave it to cook for too long, the noodles will turn to mush!

TOASTED CREAM

Prep: 10mins.   Cook Time: 2hours. SERVINGS: 16

- **1 pint heavy cream (16 fluid ounces; 473ml)**
- **1/4 teaspoon baking soda (optional)**

1. Select sous vide and Preheat to 180°F. In a medium mixing dish, combine the cream and baking soda (if using). Place zipper-lock bags or vacuum bags in a tall pitcher or jar to stand them upright, then fill the bags with cream. Remove air from zipper-lock bags using the water displacement technique, or seal vacuum bags using a vacuum sealer. Cook for 24 hours. Refrigerate cream bags before using.

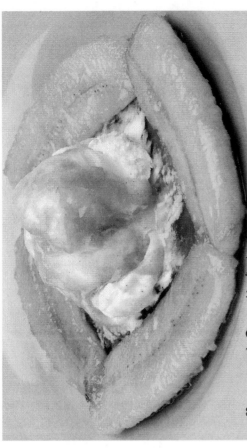

SOUS VIDE BANANAS FOSTER

Prep: 20mins.   Cook Time: 20Mins.

- **RUM SAUCE**
- **2 Tbsp Dark Rum**
- **4 Tbsp Butter**
- **1 Tsp Vanilla**
- **1/2 Cup Brown Sugar**

- **SOUS VIDE INGREDIENTS**
- **2 Bananas**
- **1 Tsp Cinnamon**
- **(Optional) 1/4 Cup Chopped Pecans**

1. In a small pot, combine all of the rum sauce ingredients and bring to a boil for 2 minutes.
2. Allow the sauce to cool.
3. Set the sous vide to Preheat the water to 145°F/63°C.
4. Peel and dice your bananas, then sprinkle with cinnamon.
5. Place the bananas in the sous vide bag, then add 3 tablespoons of your rum sauce and close. Place the remaining rum sauce in a jar for later use.
6. Cook the bananas for 25 minutes.
7. Remove the bananas from the bag and serve with vanilla ice cream if preferred. You may chill or freeze the bananas or consume them right away.
8. (Optional) For that "something extra," drizzle additional rum sauce over your dessert or quickly sear the bananas with a kitchen torch

SLOW-COOKER PIZZA

Prep: 10mins.   Cook Time: 3hours.

- **Cooking spray**
- **1 lb. pizza dough**
- **1 c. pizza sauce**
- **2 c. shredded mozzarella**
- **1/2 c. freshly grated Parmesan**
- **1/2 c. sliced pepperoni**
- **1/2 tsp. Italian seasoning**
- **pinch of crushed red pepper**
- **flakes**
- **1 tsp. Freshly chopped parsley, for garnish**

1. Coat the bottom and sides of a saucepan with nonstick cooking spray.
2. Press the pizza dough into the bottom of the pot until it reaches all sides and thoroughly covers the bottom. Spread pizza sauce over the top, leaving approximately 1" of dough around the edge. Top with cheese, pepperoni, and spices.
3. Cook on low for 3 to 4 hours, or until the crust becomes golden and the cheese melts.
4. Remove the cover and let aside to cool for 5 minutes.
5. Remove the pizza from the pot using a spatula. Garnish with parsley, then slice and serve.

47

CHERRY TOMATO MOZZARELLA SAUTE

Prep: 5mins.   Cook Time: 20Mins.   Servings: 4

- 2 teaspoons olive oil
- 1/4 cup chopped shallots
- 1 teaspoon minced fresh thyme
- 1 garlic clove, minced
- 2-1/2 cups cherry tomatoes, halved
- 1/4 teaspoon salt
- 1/4 teaspoon pepper
- 4 ounces fresh mozzarella cheese,
- cut into 1/2-inch cubes

1. In a possible cooker, Set to saute/sear on LO, heat oil, and saute shallots with thyme until tender. Cook and stir for 1 minute after adding garlic. Stir in the tomatoes, salt, and pepper, and heat through. Remove the cover and mix in the cheese.

APPLE BUTTER

Prep: 20mins.   Cook Time:10hours.   Servings: 6

- 6 lb. mixed apples, peeled, cored,
- and sliced (about 12 apples)
- 1/4 c. packed brown sugar
- 1/4 c. granulated sugar
- 2 tsp. cinnamon
- 1 tsp. pure vanilla extract
- 1/2 tsp. ground nutmeg
- 1/2 tsp. ground cloves
- 1/2 tsp. kosher salt
- 1/4 tsp. ground ginger

1. Add all of the ingredients in the pot and toss to combine, Cover and cook on low for 8 hours, or until apples are deeply brown and falling apart.
2. Blend the apples with an immersion blender or a normal blender until smooth. If using the normal blender, pause to remove the lid every so often to allow steam to escape.
3. Fill jars halfway with apple butter and set aside to cool to room temperature. Refrigerate and It can also be stored for a few weeks

48

FLOP-PROOF CHOCOLATE CAKE

Prep: 20mins.   Cook Time: 20Mins.   Servings: 8

- Cacoa Mixture
- 250 ml Boiling water
- 125 ml Oil
- 125 ml Cocoa
- 5 ml Vanilla
- Cake mixture

- 4 Eggs
- 375 ml White sugar
- 450 ml Cake Flour
- 10 ml Baking powder
- Chocolate Icing

- 125 g Woodenspoon Butter
- 500 ml Icing sugar
- 125 ml Cocoa
- 5 ml Vanilla essence
- 5 ml Hot water

1. Combine the boiling water, oil, and cocoa in a mixing bowl. Allow to cool. After it has cooled, add the vanilla essence. Set aside for now.
2. In a separate dish, whisk together the eggs and sugar until they are white and fluffy.
3. Then, Sift in the flour, baking powder, and salt and stir to combine.
4. Fold the cocoa mixture into the cake batter. Do not combine.
5. Pour the batter into two prepared 7-square inch round cake pans.
6. After then, Bake at 180°C for 25-30 minutes.
7. Next, Remove the cakes from the oven and set them aside to cool.

For the Icing

1. Combine the butter, icing, cocoa, vanilla, and boiling water until smooth and fluffy.
2. Decorate your cake any way you wish. Enjoy

FAIL-PROOF MEATLOAF

Prep: 10mins.   Cook Time: 1hours.   Servings: 8

- 1.5 lb ground meat
- 1 egg
- 1 c. Milk
- 1 c. Crumbs (bread or cracker)
- 4 tbsp brown sugar

- 4 tbsp yellow mustard
- 2/3 cup ketchup
- 1 small onion (optional)
- Salt & pepper to taste (optional)

1. Preheat the conventional oven to 350°F.
2. In a large mixing bowl, combine the beef, egg, onion, milk, and bread OR cracker crumbs. Season with salt and pepper to taste and shape into a loaf and place in the lightly greased pot.
3. In a separate small dish, add the brown sugar, mustard, and ketchup. Half of the mixture should be poured over the meatloaf. (Or more if you choose). Then, use the remaining sauce as a dipping sauce.
4. Bake the whole pot (without covering) for 1 hour, or until it is lightly brown.

49

SLOW-COOKER MASHED POTATOES

Prep: 20mins.   Cook Time: 20Mins. Servings: 10

- **3 lb. Yukon Gold potatoes**
- **1 1/2 tsp. kosher salt, plus more**
- **3/4 c. (1 1/2 sticks) unsalted butter,**
- **divided**
- **1 c. sour cream**
- **Freshly ground black pepper**

1. Firstly, Scrub and peel potatoes, then cut into 1/4" thick slices. Place potatoes in a large mixing bowl. Cover with cold water, stirring potatoes with your hands as the bowl fills with water. Return the potatoes to the bowl after draining. Repeat the procedure once or twice more until the water flows clean. Place potatoes in the pot.

2. Bring salt and 1 1/2 cups water to a boil in a kettle. Pour boiling water over potatoes. Thinly slice 1/2 cup (1 stick) butter and lay on top of potatoes. Place a sheet of parchment on top of the potatoes, then gently tuck the parchment down around the edges. (The potatoes should be completely coated.)

3. Cover and set slow cook to cook on high for 4 hours, or until potatoes are tendered. Discard the parchment. Save approximately 1/2 cup of the cooking liquid before draining the potatoes and returning them to the pot.

4. Mash potatoes with sour cream and the remaining 4 tablespoons of butter in the pot until smooth. Add cooking liquid, 1 to 2 tablespoons at a time, to loosen potatoes to the desired consistency; season with salt and pepper.

STUFFING

Prep: 15mins.   Cook Time: 4hours.   Servings: 8

- **Cooking spray for pot**
- **1/2 c. (1 stick) butter**
- **3 stalks celery, finely chopped**
- **1 medium onion, finely chopped**
- **1 tsp. fresh thyme leaves**
- **1 tsp. fresh rosemary, finely**
- **chopped**
- **1 tsp. sage, finely chopped**
- **2 large eggs, beaten**
- **2 c. low-sodium chicken broth**
- **kosher salt**
- **Freshly ground black pepper**
- **7 c. stale bread, cubed into small pieces**
- **1 tbsp. parsley, finely chopped,**
- **plus more for garnish**

1. Select saute/sear on an LO and melt butter in the pot. Once melted, add celery, onion, and herbs. Season with salt and pepper and sauté until the onions are transparent, approximately 5 minutes. After then, Remove from heat and set aside to cool.

2. Grease the bowl of the Pot and add the cubed bread. Pour the vegetable mixture, eggs, broth, and parsley over the bread. Toss to combine and cover.

3. Cook on low for 3 to 4 hours, stir after 2 hours. Before serving, sprinkle with parsley

50

CAULIFLOWER-SALSA SALAD

Prep: 10mins.   Cook Time: 10Mins. Servings: 6

- 1 medium head cauliflower
- 1 container (16 ounces) refrigerated
- fresh salsa
- 1 tablespoon garlic oil
- 1/4.teaspoon coarsely ground pepper
- 1 cup flat-leaf parsley or
- cilantro leaves

1. Cut the cauliflower into florets. Place a steamer rack in the pot over 1 inch of water. Place cauliflower on the rack. Bring the water to a boil. Steam for 6-8 minutes on a LO. Remove cauliflower and immediately immerse in freezing water. Drain and pat dry.
2. Toss cauliflower with salsa, garlic oil, pepper, and parsley in a large mixing bowl. Refrigerate for at least 30 minutes, and up to 2 hours, before serving

INDIVIDUAL FLANS

Prep: 10mins.   Cook Time: 20mis.   Servings: 2

- 2 tablespoons sweetened shredded coconut
- 2 teaspoons caramel ice cream topping
- 1 large egg
- 1 large egg yolk
- 3/4 cup half-and-half cream
- 3 tablespoons sugar
- 1/4 teaspoon vanilla extract
- Pinch ground allspice

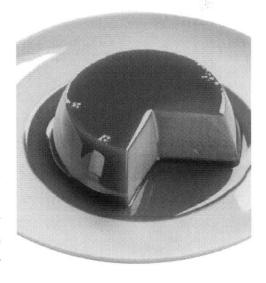

1. Divide the coconut between two ungreased 6-oz. custard cups. Drizzle with caramel topping. In a separate dish, mix together the remaining ingredients; pour into custard cups.
2. Place a steamer rack inside the pot. Fill the pot with water almost close to the top of the rack. Place the custard cups on the rack. Bring to a boil, then cover and steam for 10-12 minutes, or until a knife inserted 1 inch from the edge comes out clean.
3. Place the cups on a wire rack to cool for 10 minutes. Run a knife around the cup's rim. Unmold flans onto dessert dishes and serve warm

SOUS VIDE 'COLD' BREW COFFEE

Prep: 20mins.   Cook Time: 2hours. Servings: 6

- **1/2 cup fresh coarse ground coffee**
- **4 cups water**

1. Set the Sous Vide to 150°F/65.5°C.
2. Combine 1/2 cup coffee and 4 cups water in two mason jars or a big glass jug. Tighten lids using your fingers, being cautious not to overtighten.
3. Place in a pot for two hours.
4. When the timer goes off, take the jars from the pot and filter the coffee through regular coffee filters into a big jug.
5. Refrigerate for up to 10 day

FISH & SEAFOODS

NORTH CAROLINA SHRIMP SAUTE

Prep: 5mins.   Cook Time: 20Mins. Servings: 4

- 8 ounces uncooked linguine or
- spaghetti
- 4 tablespoons butter, divided
- 1/2 pound sliced fresh mushrooms
- 1 small green pepper, chopped
- 1/2 teaspoon salt
- 1/4 teaspoon pepper

- 1 pound uncooked shrimp
- (31-40 per pound), peeled and deveined
- 3 garlic cloves, minced
- 1/2 cup grated Romano cheese
- Chopped fresh parsley

1. Cook linguini according to package instructions; drain and keep warm.
2. Meanwhile, in a possible cooker, Select saute/sear on low, heat 2.tablespoons butter, and cook mushrooms and green pepper until soft. season with salt and pepper, and remove from the pot
3. Sauté the shrimp in the remaining butter for 2 minutes in the same cooker.
4. Cook, stirring constantly, until the shrimp become pink, about 1-2 minutes. Stir in the mushroom mixture and heat through. Serve with linguini. Sprinkle with cheese and parsley

SAUTÉED SHRIMP WITH GARLIC, LEMON, AND HERBS

Prep: 5mins.   Cook Time: 10mis.   Servings: 4

- 2 tablespoons extra-virgin olive oil
- 2 cloves garlic finely
- chopped/minced (about 1 teaspoon)
- 1 teaspoon dried oregano
- 1/2 teaspoon crushed red pepper
- (optional, more or less depending on spice preference)
- 1 – 1.5 lb. jumbo shrimp peeled and
- deveined, tail on or
- off depending on preference

- 1/4 teaspoon kosher salt more if needed
- 1/2 teaspoon black pepper
- 2 tablespoons lemon juice
- (from about 1 lemon)
- 1/4 cup dry white wine or
- chicken broth, or water in a pinch

1. Select saute/sear on low. In the pot, heat 2 tablespoons of oil. Then, Add the minced garlic (2 cloves/1 teaspoon), dried oregano (1 teaspoon), and then crushed red pepper, if using (1/2 teaspoon). Cook, uncovered, for 2-3 minutes, or until garlic is aromatic and slightly roasted but not burnt.
2. Meanwhile, pat the shrimp dry and season with kosher salt (1/2 teaspoon) and black pepper (1/2 teaspoon).
3. Add the shrimp to the the pot and cook on LO for 2 minutes on each side, or until nearly entirely cooked through and opaque.
4. Add the lemon juice and white wine (1/4 cup). Continue to cook until the liquid has almost totally reduced and thickened (approximately 2-3 minutes), covering the shrimp in a rich sauce. Transfer to a serving tray or individual plates, being sure to scoop all of the sauce from the pot on top of the shrimp before serving

SOUS VIDE SCALLOPS WITH LEMON BUTTER

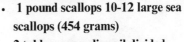

Prep: 2mins.   Cook Time: 20Mins. Servings: 4

- 1 pound scallops 10-12 large sea scallops (454 grams)
- 2 tablespoons olive oil divided
- fresh ground black pepper and
- Salt to taste
- 2 tablespoons unsalted butter (divided)
- 3 cloves garlic minced
- (or 1 tablespoon minced garlic)
- 2 tablespoons lemon juice
- 1 tablespoon chopped parsley
- Optional for serving

1. Fill the pot with water and set the sous vide to 123°F/51°C.
2. Remove any tough muscle from the scallops' sides.
3. Season the scallops with salt, pepper, and 1 tablespoon of olive oil.
4. Place the scallops in a large resealable bag or vacuum seal bag in a single layer. (Make sure to place it in one layer. If your bag is too small, use.many bags).
5. Then, Seal the bag using the "water displacement" technique or a vacuum sealer.
6. Set the timer for 30 minutes after the temperature has reached the target temperature. Make certain that the scallops are thoroughly submerged in water.
7. When the timer goes off, Transfer the bag to an ice bath. Leave for 15 minutes (or chill in the refrigerator for approximately 1 hour).
8. When the scallops have cooled, take them from the bag and wipe them dry with paper towels (wet scallops will not sear correctly).
9. Set the sear/saute to high and add the remaining 1 tablespoon olive oil and 1 tablespoon butter.
10. When the butter has stopped foaming, add the scallops and fry for 30seconds on one side (until a golden crust develops below), then turn and cook for another 30 seconds until gently browned. Remove from the pot and place on a dish.
11. In the same pot, combine the remaining 1 tablespoon of butter and garlic. Then, Cook for approximately 1 minute, or until aromatic.
12. Add the lemon juice and scrape out any browned pieces. After then cook the sauce for around 2 minutes.
13. Toss the cooked scallops with the sauce in the pot.
14. Garnish with parsley if desired.

BAKED SALMON

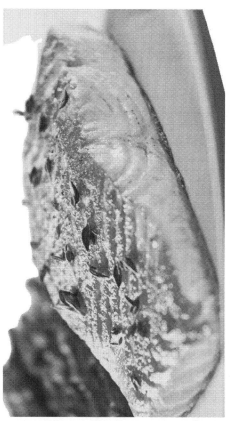

Prep: 5mins.   Cook Time: 10Mins. Servings: 4

- **4 salmon filets, skin-on**
- **(about 6–8 ounces each)**
- **2 tablespoons high-heat oil,**
- **such as avocado oil or canola oil**
- **Kosher salt and**
- **Freshly-cracked black pepper**
- **Fresh lemon wedges**

1. Allow the salmon to sit on the counter for 15-30 minutes.
2. Preheat the conventional oven to 450°F. Then, Line the pot with a baking sheet.
3. Dry the salmon filets on both sides with paper towels. After then, Place the salmon skin-side down on the prepared baking sheet. If the edges of the salmon filets are very thin, tuck them under a little for even cooking.
4. Brush oil on all sides of the fish (except the bottom). Season each filet generously with salt and black pepper, as well as any other dry seasonings you want.
5. Bake at 135-140°F for 4-6 minutes per half-inch thickness. You can also test for doneness by sticking a fork or knife into the salmon and turning it slightly; the fish should be opaque and flake easily.
6. Remove the salmon from the oven and place it on a clean serving plate, skin behind. Sprinkle each filet with a generous squeeze of lemon juice, as well as any additional fresh herbs or sauce that you desire. Then serve warm and enjoy!

BAKED SHRIMP

Prep: 5mins.   Cook Time: 2mis.   Servings: 4

- **1 pound shrimp, peeled and**
- **deveined (tails on or off)**
- **1 tablespoon avocado oil**
- **(or your preferred high-heat oil)**
- **Kosher salt and**
- **Freshly-ground black pepper, to taste**

1. Preheat the conventional oven to broil.Place the baking rack approximately 5 inches away from the top heating element.
2. Then, Place the shrimp in a large mixing bowl and pat dry with paper towels. Toss the shrimp in the oil until uniformly covered.
3. Line the pot with a baking sheet. Then, Place the shrimp on top in an equal layer. (Make sure the shrimp do not overlap.) Season liberally with salt, pepper, and any other preferred ingredients.
4. Then, Broil for 2 minutes, or until the shrimp are bright reddish-pink and opaque. After then, Remove from the oven and place on a serving plate.
5. Serve warm. Transfer to a covered container and refrigerate for up to 2 days, or freeze for up to 3 months.

FRESH HERB AND MEDITERRANEAN-STYLE STEAMED SALMON WITH LEMON

Prep: 2mins.   Cook Time: 20Mins. Servings: 4

- 1 yellow onion, halved and sliced
- 4 green onions (spring onions),
- trimmed and sliced lengthwise, divided
- 1 lb skin-on salmon fillet
- (such as wild Alaskan), cut into 4 portions
- Kosher salt
- Black pepper
- 1 tsp/ 1.67 g ground coriander
- 1 tsp/2.6 g ground cumin
- ½ tsp/ 1.33 g Aleppo pepper
- 4 to 5 garlic cloves, chopped
- Extra virgin olive oil
- A large handful fresh parsley (about 28 g)
- 1 lemon, thinly sliced
- ½ cup white wine
- (or you can use water or
- low-sodium broth, if you prefer)

1. Cut a big piece of parchment (approximately 2 feet long) and set it in the middle of the pot.
2. Place the sliced yellow onions and part of the green onions on the bottom of a parchment-lined pot. Arrange salmon on top, skin side-down. Then, season with kosher salt and black pepper to taste.
3. In a small bowl, combine the coriander, cumin, and Aleppo pepper. Coat the top of the salmon with the spice mixture. Next, Drizzle with a little extra virgin olive oil.
4. Arrange the garlic, parsley, and remaining green onions on top of the salmon (spread evenly). Arrange lemon slices on top.
5. Pour in the white wine, followed by another dab of extra virgin olive oil.
6. Fold the parchment paper over to cover the salmon and seal the edges. Cover the pot.
7. Set the steam on Hi and cook for 5 minutes (do not uncover). Cook for another 8 minutes, covered, on low heat.
8. Then, Remove from heat and let aside for 5 minutes.
9. Lastly, Remove the lid and serve straight from the pot.

BAKED FISH

Prep:10 mins.   Cook Time: 20Mins. Servings:1

- 1 large whole fish
- (such as mahi mahi, sea bass, or
- branzino), scaled and gutted
- 1–2 tablespoons olive oil
- 1 large clove garlic, peeled and minced
- 1 lemon, halved
- handful of fresh herbs
- (such as rosemary and thyme)
- sea salt,
- freshly-cracked black pepper and
- garlic powder

1. Preheat the conventional oven to 450°F. Coat the pot with cooking spray.

2. Once you're ready to cook, give your fish one more thorough rinse before patting it dry with paper towels. Using a sharp knife, delicately score the top of the fish in 1-inch-apart diagonal lines.

3. Brush the oil liberally on both sides of the fish. Brush the interior cavity with oil as well.

4. Slice half of the lemon into slices and insert them, along with the garlic and herbs, into the cavity of the fish (making sure the garlic is fully tucked in and not exposed).

5. Season the outside of the fish liberally with sea salt, black pepper, and garlic powder.

6. Place the pot immediately in the preheated oven and roast for 18-20 minutes (cooking time may vary based on the size/variety of the fish).

7. Remove from the oven and equally pour the juice of the remaining lemon half over the top of the fish.

8. Serve warm and enjoy!

LEMON GARLIC SOUS VIDE COD

Prep: 5mins.   Cook Time: 30Mins. Servings: 3

- 3 cod fillets 12 oz or
- 340 g total, fresh or thawed
- 1/2 tablespoon olive oil
- 1 lemon cut into slices
- 1/4 teaspoon garlic powder
- 1/4 teaspoon paprika
- 1/4 teaspoon salt or to taste
- 1/8 teaspoon ground black pepper
- or to taste chopped parsley
- optional for serving

1. Fill the pot with water and set the Sous Vide to 132°F (55.6°C).
2. In a small mixing bowl, combine garlic powder, paprika, salt, and pepper.
3. Rub olive oil all over the cod. Then, spread the seasoning mixture on all sides of each cod fillet.
4. In a zip-top bag, combine sliced lemon and seasoned cod. Arrange them in a single layer. (A single layer ensures perfect cooking; if your bag is too small, use many bags.)
5. Seal all but one corner of the bag. Place it slowly in the water bath, making sure that everything below the zip-line is submerged. Then close the remaining part of the bag.
6. Cook the cod in a heated water bath for 30 minutes. (If the cod is not entirely immersed in the water, use kitchen metal tongs to keep it in place.
7. Remove the bag from the water and carefully remove the cod. (Cooked cod tends to come apart extremely easily). Serve immediately with optional chopped parsley

SOUS VIDE HALIBUT

Prep: 5mins.   Cook Time: 45Mins. Servings: 4

- **1 pound fresh halibut filet**
- **1 clove garlic minced**
- **2 tablespoons unsalted butter**
- **salt to taste**
- **pepper to taste**
- **4 sprigs fresh thyme optional**
- **5 slices lemon optional**
- **For Searing**
- **1 tablespoon unsalted butter**
- **chopped parsley optional for serving**

1. Fill the pot with water and set the Sous Vide to 132°F (55.6°C).
2. Season both sides with salt and pepper. On top of each filet, sprinkle with chopped garlic, thyme, and butter.
3. In a zip-lock bag, combine the sliced lemon and seasoned halibut filets. Arrange them in a single layer. (It's important to boil them in one layer; if your bag isn't large enough, use several bags.)
4. Seal all but one corner of the bag. Place it slowly in the water, making sure that everything below the zip-line is submerged. Then close the rest of the bag.
5. Cook the halibut filets in heated water for 30-45 minutes for 1-inch fillets or 45-60 minutes for 1.5-inch fillets. (Make sure any portion of the fish is totally submerged in water; if your bag is half-floating, use kitchen metal tongs to keep it in place.)

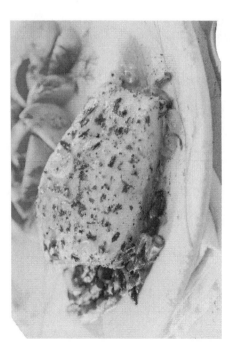

6. Remove the bag from the water and carefully remove the halibut from it. (Cooked halibut tends to come apart quite easily; move to a plate).
7. Allow the halibut to chill for approximately 10 minutes in the refrigerator. Then, use paper towels, and thoroughly dry the area.
8. Set sear/sauté to high and add butter. When the butter has melted, gently place the halibut filets in the pot, presenting-side down. After then, Sear for 30 seconds, just to brown the surface. Remove from the pot immediately.
9. Serve with lemon wedges and minced parsley.

SOUS VIDE LOBSTER TAILS

Prep:15mins.   Cook Time: 45Mins. Servings:2

- **2 lobster tails**
- **2 tablespoons unsalted butter**
- **cut into 6-8 small pieces (Plus more for dipping)**
- **1 clove minced garlic**
- **1/4 teaspoon salt**
- **1/4 teaspoon black pepper**
- **2 large lemons cut into slices**
- **chopped parley optional**

1. Fill the pot with water and set the Sous Vide to 140°F (60°C).
2. Then, Cut along the middle of the top shell, towards the tail fins (do not cut through the end). Make sure to cut in a straight line.
3. Separate the flesh from the shell using the handle end of a spoon, then carefully pull the shell out. While the end of the shell is still connected to the meat, gently pull it up and out.
4. Season the meat with salt, pepper, and chopped garlic. Then press the meat back into the shell.
5. Add butter pieces on top.
6. In a big zip-lock bag, arrange lemon slices in a single layer. Then, serve with seasoned lobster tails on top.
7. Except for one corner, seal the bag. Place it slowly in the water bath, making sure that everything below the zip-line is submerged. Then close the rest of the bag.
8. Cook the lobster for 45 minutes to an hour.
9. When the timer goes off, take the lobster tail from the bag. As lobster tails may be eaten immediately after sous vide cooking, there is no need for searing.
10. Optional: Lift the meat up and out of the shell for an amazing appearance.
11. Serve immediately with lemon wedges and heated butter for dipping.

HAPPY COOKING

"Cooking demands attention, patience, and above all, a respect for the gifts of the earth. It is a form of worship, a way of giving thanks."

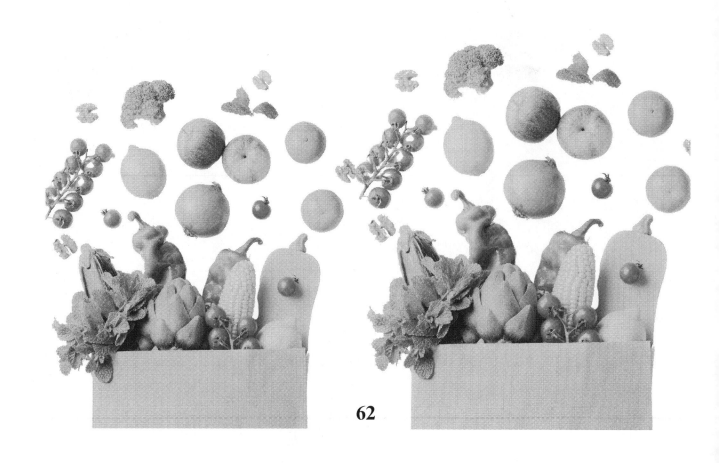

NINJA MEAL PLANNER

Weekly. Guided. Planning

MY DAILY FOOD PLAN

	BREAKFAST	LUNCH	DINNER	SNACKS
MON				
TUE				
WED				
THU				
FRI				
SAT				
SUN				

WEEK 1

MY DAILY FOOD PLAN

	BREAKFAST	LUNCH	DINNER	SNACKS
MON				
TUE				
WED				
THU				
FRI				
SAT				
SUN				

WEEK 2

MY DAILY FOOD PLAN

	BREAKFAST	LUNCH	DINNER	SNACKS
MON				
TUE				
WED				
THU				
FRI				
SAT				
SUN				

WEEK 3

MY DAILY FOOD PLAN

	BREAKFAST	LUNCH	DINNER	SNACKS
MON				
TUE				
WED				
THU				
FRI				
SAT				
SUN				

WEEK 4

MY DAILY FOOD PLAN

	BREAKFAST	LUNCH	DINNER	SNACKS
MON				
TUE				
WED				
THU				
FRI				
SAT				
SUN				

WEEK 5

Made in United States
Orlando, FL
08 December 2024

55216262R00039